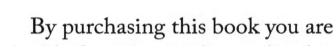

ISBN 978-0-266-98107-7
PIBN 10918865

This book is a reproduction of an important historical work. Forgotten Books uses state-of-the-art technology to digitally reconstruct the work, preserving the original format whilst repairing imperfections present in the aged copy. In rare cases, an imperfection in the original, such as a blemish or missing page, may be replicated in our edition. We do, however, repair the vast majority of imperfections successfully; any imperfections that remain are intentionally left to preserve the state of such historical works.

How to avoid a Fuel Bill next Fall...

IF you were about to incur some new financial obligation, and you were privileged to make the annual payment involved at the time of the year you preferred, would you choose the Spring or the Fall?

Having in mind your present peak of fixed expense at the latter part of the year, you would, in all probability, express a preference for the Spring.

If you put it off until you actually need heat, then the cost of the coal will become a Fall expense — coming when important other expenses have to be borne. But if you buy your coal in advance, in the Spring, you shift that obligation to a time when it can be more easily met.

As a further advantage, Old Company dealers make a lower seasonal price on coal bought during the Spring.

Old Company's Lehigh Anthracite is a notably high-grade hard coal, slow and even-burning, flexible under draft-control, and requires but minimum attention. The experience of a century endorses it to the householder as the ideal home-heating fuel.

> *Tune in on the*
> OLD
> COMPANY'S
> SINGERS
> *with*
> SIGMUND
> SPAETH
> Sunday Even'g
> *at 7 P.M.*
> WEAF and
> Associated
> Stations

OLD COMPANY'S
LEHIGH ANTHRACITE

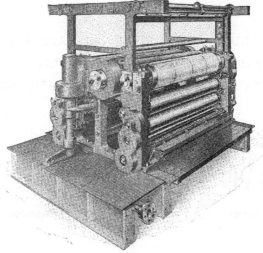

BETWEEN
The
LINES

SUB-FRESHMAN Day turned out to be an Alumni Day in miniature. Lehigh men for miles around brought carloads of likely looking youngsters. Enough materi-al for a dozen teams.

* *. *

The banquet for the visitors looked like an Alumni Dinner if every-one. could look as young as he feels. Only the sub-frosh didn't know the songs.

* * *

Still, as they say in Lehighton, "Dot ain't such a difference."

DO you feel tired and nervous? Are you irritable, worn-out and lacking in pep? Do you hate to go to bed at night and hate to get up in the morning? Do you take cream in your coffee? Does your heart beat and. the blood · flow through your arteries?

* * *

If so, you should be in Bethlehem on June 8. Dr. Lehigh's famous elixir is guaranteed to cure any and all disorders arising from boredom, overwork, separation from friends and taking oneself too seriously.

* * *

Big free sample, June 8, 1929.

* * *

All contributions to the Alumni Fund are deductible from your in-come tax.

BASEBALL

May	4	Lafayette*
May	7	Penn*
May	8	C. C. N. Y.
May	11	Lafayette
May	15	Rutgers
May	18	Lafayette*
June	7	Muhlenberg
June	8	Villanova

LACROSSE

May	4	Stevens
May	11	Swarthmore*
May	18	Montclair A. C.

TRACK

May	4	Lafayette*
May	11	Rutgers
May	18	Union*

TENNIS

May	3	Swarthmore
May	4	Rutgers*
May	9	Georgetown
May	11	Yale*
May	17	Dartmouth
May	20	Haverford
May	21	Lafayette

* Games away.

LEHIGH ALUMNI BULLETIN

Published monthly, October to July inclusive, by the Alumni Association of Lehigh University, Inc., Bethlehem, Pa.
Printed by Times Publishing Co., Bethlehem, Pa.
Subscription Price, $2.00 a Year
Member of Intercollegiate Alumni Extension Service
Entered as second-class matter at Bethlehem, Penna., Post-office
A. E. BUCHANAN, JR., '18, *Editor*   J. W. MAXWELL, '26, *Asst. Editor*

VOLUME 16	MAY, 1929 ·	NUMBER 8

LEHIGH ALUMNI BULLETIN

MAY, 1929

On Entering the Million-Dollar-a-Year Class

LEHIGH'S operating budget for the next fiscal year, just approved by the Board of Trustees, totals well over a million dollars. Even in these remarkable days, in which the million is a familiar unit, used as glibly as the dozen or the ton, it will surprise many to learn that the annual expenditures of Lehigh University run into seven figures. It was accepted as a matter of course by the Trustees, who have watched the scale of our operations double during the six years of President Richards' administration. They expected the budget to exceed a million dollars; they would have been disappointed if it had not, and they anticipate, with matter-of-fact assurance, continued growth at a comparable rate.

AS LEHIGH stockholders, we alumni have every reason to appreciate the broad visioned leadership of the Trustees who are directing this progress. We cannot give too much credit to the President who plans the budget and who has directed operations so wisely that each year has added moderately to an accumulated surplus which is now available for the extensive alterations which become desirable with the occupation of the James Ward Packard Laboratory of Electrical and Mechanical Engineering. Over one hundred thousand dollars will be expended this summer to adapt for more effective use the facilities of Packer Hall, the Chemistry Laboratory, Williams Hall and the Physics Building. Here is just one concrete evidence of the splendid accomplishment that results from the combination of a Packard's generosity with an able administration of high purpose and firm resolve.

THE impressiveness of Lehigh's growth is not in its mere magnitude. The "bigger and better" appeal per se is shallow, and its edge is dulled from excessive use. There would be only superficial pride in the acquisition of new buildings and improved physical plant if there were not ample evidence that these facilities pay for themselves many times over by improving the quality of Lehigh's product. There would be little satisfaction in turning out graduates if industry and business were not aggressively eager to absorb them. The prestige of our Faculty would be an unconvincing boast if each man were not forging ahead in his own field, contributing to human knowledge, keeping abreast with the pioneers of thought and inspiring youth to richer and more useful lives.

IT IS with no spirit of braggadocio, therefore, that Lehigh announces her entry to the million-dollar-a-year class. There is no ballyhoo for "bigger and better budgets." Instead there is abundant reassurance that her policies are sound and her plans feasible; there is the calm assumption that another decade may demand another doubling of operating expense and there is abiding confidence in Lehigh's fitness to keep step with the vanguard of American industry and American culture.

In brief, Lehigh's remarkable growth is merely the vindication of the lifelong policy that has animated her progress and guided her destiny—Education for Service.

In Memory of THE good that a man does
C. K. Baldwin, '95 lives after him, but more
than that, the residue of good
subdivides and grows until the aggregate of good is
greater than the fondest hopes of him who created the
nucleus. So may it be with the C. Kemble Baldwin
Foundation for Research and Instruction in Aeronautics, established in memory of that highly revered member of the class of '95 by his loyal widow.

"Mr. Baldwin had two great hobbies," she explained. "One was aviation and the other was Lehigh.
I know he would be pleased if he could do something
for both of them." Thus came about the $25,000 endowment fund which will yield an annual income to
support a research fellow in some division of science or
technology pertaining to aeronautics. This handsome
gift is to be supplemented by Baldwin's extensive and
unusually complete library of aeronautical books. Thus
the memory of another loyal son of Lehigh, cherished
as a friend by his contemporaries, is perpetuated for
generations who may look back with gratitude on the
part he played, through his college, in the conquest
of the air.

"Gives She ABOUT three years ago, a young
Gladly ..." man wandered into the Alumni
Office, bearing a letter of introduction
from an alumnus and announcing his intention of entering Lehigh. He had come 1000 miles from home;
had less than a hundred dollars to his name and very
slim prospects of receiving financial assistance from
home. The tuition had just been raised to four hundred dollars and it seemed kindest to advise him not
to undertake the long grind that might overtax him
physically, but to return home where he could attend
a local college while living with his family. He listened
attentively, appreciated the advice and apologetically
announced that he guessed he'd try it anyway. To
make a long story short, he did try it and what is more,
he did it. Enrolled in a difficult engineering course,
he has maintained good averages, participated in activities, captained a varsity team, made honorary societies and with it all, waited table, peddled books and
devised various ingenious ways of balancing his budget. He is only one of the fine, determined youngsters
who are winning their diplomas in the face of similar
obstacles. And when Lehigh finds such a one in her
midst she gives him every possible assistance.

From September 1 to March 1 of this college year,
203 boys have been helped, through scholarships and
loans to the extent of $66,117. Sixty-eight seniors,
fifty-eight juniors, forty sophomores and thirty-seven
freshmen have received financial assistance, either in
the form of free scholarships, deferred tuition scholarships (repaid after graduation) or loans from the
Coxe, President's and Frank Williams ('87) Funds.
All scholarships are awarded on the basis of three
factors: Need for assistance, scholastic record (C or
better) and character and personality.

It is seldom, if ever, that a boy who really wants a
Lehigh degree and who is capable of satisfactory work
finds it necessary to forego his ambition on account of
poverty. The ideals of the founder are too thoroughly
entrenched in Old South Mountain to permit otherwise.

Good Work by EVERY now and then, youth
the Lehigh Clubs loses patience with us old
stick-in-the-muds and reveals its
contempt for our stodgy conservatism and our misguided conceptions. Just at the moment, there are
echoes "far above Cayuga's waters" of the frank opinion of undergraduates that Cornell athletics would be
all right if the alumni would just stop messing with
them. It wasn't so long ago that Lehigh students were
advising alumni that the latter's tendency to get all hot
and bothered about losing football games to Lafayette
was puerile and unworthy. More recently, undergraduate opinion expressed through the *Brown and White*
has been frankly skeptical of the vaunted "spirit" of
Lehigh alumni because of the failure of the Mustard
and Cheese Club to negotiate out-of-town performances
under the auspices of the various Lehigh clubs.

Actually, of course, the difficulty was due, not to lack
of "spirit" but to the possession of too much common
sense by the Alumni Clubs to commit themselves to
terms which obviously precluded any reasonable chance
of making the venture self-supporting. As soon as the
boys scaled down their ambitions to a rational level, the
Philadelphia Club promptly demonstrated its willingness to support a show and sponsored the production
of "The Bad Man" on May 2.

All of which is merely preliminary to the reflection
that this has been a productive year among the Lehigh
Clubs. A number of significant events have been sponsored in different cities. With very few exceptions, the
meetings have been more frequent and more interesting than usual. The Clubs are doing a good job for
Lehigh and having a bully time doing it.

Something A Lehigh ANOTHER enterprise by the
Club Can Do Lehigh Club of Philadelphia deserves mention as a novelty and a practice that might appeal to other alumni
groups. With the object of interesting desirable students in Lehigh, subscriptions to the *Brown and White*
and the BULLETIN have been taken for about thirty of
the leading high and preparatory schools in and around
Philadelphia. Preliminary correspondence with each
school indicated that they would be glad to receive the
publications and would see that students were given
access to them regularly.

Of course, not many Lehigh Clubs can boast a treasury like "Berny's," but since both publications are
glad to co-operate by giving the lowest possible rates
for group subscriptions, the idea is passed along for
the consideration of those who are interested in increasing the quota of "local" boys at Lehigh.

"Come All Ye Loyal Lehigh Men
And We'll Whoop it up with all Our Might...."

ONCE more the feel of June is in the air and Alumni Day begins to loom as the high spot on thousands of Lehigh calendars. June 8 is the official date, although the festivities begin on Friday the seventh and continue in full swing through to Commencement on Tuesday the eleventh. Seven to eleven—lucky days for lucky boys who have grown up without growing old and for old ones who want to grow young.

Even the regulars who never miss an Alumni Day will find some new sights to see—the new Library and the James Ward Packard Laboratory. And every opportunity will be provided for obtaining an eye-full, for the Alumni Meeting will be held in the auditorium of the new laboratory on Saturday morning. Luncheon will be served in the Commons anytime between twelve and two so that those who want to avoid the rush can do so by coming early.

The reunion classes, a live-wire aggregation this year —the '14's and the '9's, and '28 in the bargain—will take the center of the stage in the afternoon, with the costume parade across the campus to Taylor Field and the ball game. Villanova is scheduled as the victim for our heavy hitters this year.

The big alumni dinner will be held as usual in the Hotel Bethlehem at 7 o'clock Friday evening. Alumni ladies will dine with faculty wives in the Fountain Room at the same time. A painless program of dyed-in-the-wool Lehigh entertainment is scheduled and strenuous efforts are being made to provide merriment galore with a minimum of congestion and confusion. On Saturday evening, of course, the reunion classes will banquet in their own selected environments and decide the really important affairs of Lehigh to their own satisfaction.

Alumni Day, 1929, is to be just a big open-house for every Lehigh man who can climb the New Street hill. Alma Mater waits to welcome home her boys.

A Sight For Sore Eyes, Old Eyes, Young Eyes, LEHIGHS!
Here she is in all her glory, the Old Lady of Ten Thousand Beaux.
She was snapped from the air by Eddie Clement, '16, of the Airmap Corporation of America.

Two Hundred and Fifty Sub-Freshmen Get Taste of Life at Lehigh by Visit to Campus on April 27

MORE than two hundred and fifty high and preparatory school boys from all sections of the East, prospective Lehigh freshmen for next Fall, were the guests of the University for the Annual Sub-Freshman Day on April 27. This is by far the greatest number of boys who have ever attended an event of this kind on our campus and while the tangible results will not show until next Fall, it is reasonable to expect to find a large proportion of them battling with the sophomores on Founder's Day next October. They were all invited to visit Lehigh through alumni, undergraduates or other friends of the University so they are all boys who are believed to be first class Lehigh calibre. As would be expected, there were a goodly number of promising athletes among them, ones who are good "students" as well as being good backs, pitchers or hurdlers!

Since many of these boys arrived on Saturday morning and stayed until sometime Sunday, they had a good chance to catch the Lehigh spirit. There were enough activities to give them a typical cross-section of life on the campus, including a baseball and football game, a tennis match, a dinner with alumni, and a Mustard and Cheese show. Classes were in session as usual when many of them arrived so they had a glimpse of this all-important side of Lehigh life.

The baseball game with the Army turned out to be ideal for just such an occasion. It had more thrills packed into its eleven innings than any game seen on the home diamond in a decade and after tieing the score twice, Lehigh won in a hair-raising finish. If it had been purposely staged, the game could not have given the sub-freshmen a better demonstration of Lehigh fight and spirit. This was followed by an abbreviated football game by Austy's aspirants who were completing their four weeks' of spring practice.

The scene of activity then adjourned to the ballroom of the Hotel Bethlehem which is familiar to many alumni as the scene of the annual banquet in June. Here the boys were the guests of alumni, undergraduates and faculty members and the dinner rivalled the alumni gatherings in more ways than one. The boys were given a true conception of what Lehigh offers and what she stands for by Cullen Ganey, '20, president of the Lehigh Home Club, Okey, Dr. Richards and Austy. Humorous talks were given by A. W. Palmer, of the Haverford Preparatory School, and Bill Crowell, of Philadelphia, former All-American of Swarthmore and now one of the foremost football officials in the East. An orchestra and quartet of the musical clubs did their bit to make the evening a lively one. With close to four

hundred men and boys present, the ballroom was filled to overflowing so that the balcony had to be pressed into service. While the majority of the alumni present were from Bethlehem and vicinity, several of the other clubs were represented by one or more members.

The dinner was ended early enough to enable the boys to see a goodly portion of "The Bad Man," the Mustard and Cheese Club's current production, which was staged in Drown Hall. The majority of the boys stayed over night as the guests of the fraternities, some houses acting as hosts to almost twenty men.

While Austy is commonly thought of as Lehigh's football coach, too much credit cannot be given him for the success of this sub-freshman day. Instead of his assisting the Home Club in preparing for the affair, the conditions were reversed and the Home Club really assisted him. Sword and Crescent and Cyanide and the fraternities did everything in their power to work with Austy.

Another Big Construction Job Credited to Lehigh Talent

To the long list of big construction projects directed by Lehigh engineers is added the Neville Island, Pa., cement, iron and coke plant described in the following extract from a letter by Charles G. Thornburg, '09, who is chief engineer of the Rust Engineering Co. of Pittsburgh, Pa.

Our company is now completing a large cement, blast furnace and coke plant job for the Davison Coke and Iron Co., at Neville Island, Pa. The operations are nearly 100 per cent Lehigh. The writer, as chief engineer, had charge of the design of all the cement plant and blast furnace structures. Agthe, '09, was the engineer in charge for Allis Chalmers Co., who furnished the cement plant machinery. Kennedy, '12, is works manager for Davison Coke and Iron Co.; Schreiber, '15, is superintendent of the Coke Plant. Saeger, '12, is superintendent of the cement plant. The McClintic-Marshall Co., with their Lehigh men, have furnished us with the structural steel, and Dan Berg, '05, through the Dravo-Doyle Co., has furnished power plant equipment.

CHARLES G. THORNBURG, '09

Professor Barker, newly appointed head of the Department of Electrical Engineering, looks over his future headquarters, the James Ward Packard Laboratory, with President Richards.

This looks like the setting for a big swimming meet but it is really one of the features of the fourth annual welding symposium held on the campus on April 8. It was a demonstration of under water steel cutting under the direction of L. F. Hagglund, '17, who is with Merritt Chapman and Scott. Several hundred technical men attended this symposium which consisted of addresses on new developments in this field, and tests and demonstrations of various types and processes of welding.

Colonel Thomlinson Relieves Colonel McCammon as Head of Lehigh R. O. T. C.

By order of the President of the United States, Lieutenant Colonel Matthew H. Thomlinson, Infantry, will be relieved from his present assignment and duty in the Office of the Chief of Infantry at Washington, D. C., on or about August 15, 1929, when he will report to Lehigh University as Professor and Head of the Department of Military Science and Tactics in charge of the instruction in the Reserve Officers Training Corps. Colonel Thomlinson replaces Colonel McCammon, who has headed the R. O. T. C. at Lehigh for the past five years and has successfully maintained the high standards of the Department of Military Science and Tactics. Coming at a time when the Department was housed in Christmas Hall with most unattractive and meager facilities, he has seen it grow in student enrollment and in its facilities for instruction. A few years ago the building formerly occupied by the Commons was remodeled to convert it into an Armory. The building is now very well adapted to the uses to which it is put. The friends of Colonel McCammon will follow his further progress with much interest. He will join his regiment, the 38th Infantry, at Fort Douglas.

Colonel Thomlinson was born July 10, 1882. He entered the United States Military Academy at West Point in 1900 and graduated therefrom in 1904. From 1915 to 1918 he was Instructor in the Department of Tactics at West Point; in 1920 he was detailed to General Service Schools at Fort Leavenworth, from which he graduated the following year, after which he was retained for one year as an instructor; in 1926 he graduated from the Army War College at Washington and since that time has been in the Office of the Chief of Infantry of the General Staff of the Army.

New Department Established for Upkeep of Lehigh's Plant

RECOGNIZING the tremendous increase in the responsibilities of keeping the rapidly growing physical plant of the University in first-class condition, the Board of Trustees has created a new department, known as the Department of Buildings and Grounds. Mr. Andrew Willard Litzenberger, of Bethlehem, was appointed to take charge of this Department with the title of Supervising Architect of the University. In this position Mr. Litzenberger will have full charge of the maintenance, care and policing of the University grounds and buildings, including the power and heating plant, reporting directly to the President of the University. This reorganization was precipitated by the recent death of J. C. Cranmer, former superintendent of buildings and grounds.

A. W. Litzenberger
Newly appointed Supervising Architect

Mr. Litzenberger was born in Philadelphia on April 9, 1891. He is a graduate of the old Central High School of Bethlehem. After leaving the High School he pursued a two-year special course in the School of Architecture at the University of Pennsylvania, from which he received a certificate, after which he worked for two years as a draftsman with Jacoby and Weishampel, Architects of Allentown. Following this connection he accepted a position with the Bethlehem Steel Corporation where he served for six years in various work of standardization, foreign construction work, and domestic sales work, and for the last ten years as Senior Architect in charge of design and supervision of building construction for the Corporation. Through the courtesy of E. G. Grace, '99, President of the Bethlehem Steel Corporation, Mr. Litzenberger was given a leave of absence from the Corporation to act as Superintendent of Construction of the new Packard Engineering Laboratory and the new Library on the University campus so that he has actually been in the service of the University since May 1, 1928. His work in charge of the new buildings has commanded the respect of University officers and has demonstrated effectively his ability to handle the varied problems for which he will hereafter be responsible.

Prof. Miller A Delegate to Geological Congress

Dr. Benjamin L. Miller, Professor of Geology, has been selected by the Geological Society of America as an official delegate to the International Geological Congress to convene at Pretoria, South Africa, during the summer months. This congress meets tri-annually and is attended by delegates from every civilized nation. Prof. Miller attended the last session, which was held in Madrid in 1926.

J. W. Barker, of M.I.T., Named to Head
Dept. of Electrical Engineering at Lehigh

AT A MEETING of the Board of Trustees on April 15, Professor Joseph Warren Barker, of the Department of Electrical Engineering of the Massachusetts Institute of Technology, was appointed to succeed the late William Esty as Professor and Head of the Department of Electrical Engineering and Director of the Curriculum in Electrical Engineering, to be effective as soon as Professor Barker can report to the University for duty. Professor Barker's appointment marks the happy ending of a search for "just the right man" that involved a literal combing of the country's qualified electrical engineers. Never was a man more assiduously sought for such a post. All who have met Professor Barker believe that the right man is coming to the right place.

Professor Barker was born June 17, 1891, at Lawrence, Mass. After graduating from the Rockford, Ill., High School he entered the University of Chicago, where he remained a year, when he transferred to the Massachusetts Institute of Technology. He graduated from the Institute with the degree of Bachelor of Science in Electrical Engineering in 1916. Immediately thereafter he was appointed as Second Lieutenant in the Coast Artillery Corps of the Regular Army. During his army service he studied at the Coast Artillery School at Fort Monroe, Va., and the Artillery School at Fort Sill, Okla. At various times he was an Instructor in certain of the Army schools. In a short time after Professor Barker joined the Army he attained his Major's commission. During the war he was in command of troops for various periods and after the armistice he was appointed a member of the War Damage Board of the Peace Commission working in cooperation with the United States Department of State and he was for a time Adjutant General of the American Armies in Paris, cooperating in the task of returning our soldiers to America. Following this service he was detained as an officer in charge of civilian relations of the American Army of Occupation in Germany, where he served for about three years. He also cooperated as a staff officer in charge of the repatriation of General Haller's Polish Army. Upon his return to America Major Barker served for a year as Artillery Engineering Officer in charge of Power Plants and Signal Installation around the Boston Harbor, after which he was assigned to the Coast Artillery School for a year, from whence he was detailed to take graduate work in Electrical Engineering at the Massachusetts Institute of Technology, from which he received the degree of Master of Science in 1925. At various times during his service in the Army he conducted investigations of a scientific nature to improve the practices in the

Professor J. W. Barker

Coast Artillery and his thesis for his master's degree was one of similar character; all of these investigations are confidential and are in the archives of the War Department.

When he received his master's degree Major Barker was offered an associate professorship in the Department at the Institute if he would resign his commission. This he agreed to do and since that time he has been a professor in the department in charge of the administrative responsibilities connected with all undergraduate instruction and of certain outside relations maintained by the Institute with technical industries. Recently Professor Barker has had charge of certain research work in the field of electrical illumination that was done at the Institute of Technology in cooperation with the National Research Council. Lehigh men generally

will be interested to know that Professor Barker's appointment to Lehigh was enthusiastically sponsored by the University's former Professor, William S. Franklin, and by a score of prominent electrical engineers in the highest industrial and academic circles.

To Study Welds by X-Ray

Dr. Gilbert E. Doan, '19, assistant professor of metallurgy, has been engaged for important research work at the naval research laboratory at Anacostia, D. C., from June to September. His work will consist of radiographic examination of steel castings and welds by means of gamma rays from radium. As far as is known, this will be the first work of this kind undertaken in this country.

Alumni Active in Detroit Club Project

Several Lehigh alumni are actively engaged in the affairs of the new Intercollegiate Alumni Club, Detroit, which plans to erect a modern clubhouse in the center of Detroit's business district. Fifteen years ago the Intercollegiate Association was formed as a luncheon club and, among those most active in this organization, was a Lehigh man, Charles G. Heilman, '10, who at present is a member of the Board of Governors of the new club. Last December it was decided to change the name to the Intercollegiate Alumni Club with the objective of building a clubhouse. Membership at present writing is over six hundred and the number is constantly climbing. Construction of the clubhouse is expected to start early this Fall. Three other Lehigh alumni have joined the club: Earle F. Johnson, '07, Dixon H. Kirkpatrick, '17, and George W. Landrus, '04.

The cast of "The Bad Man," the forty-fifth annual production of the Mustard and Cheese Club. Two performances were given on the campus and a third at the Bellevue-Stratford Hotel for the Philadelphia Lehigh Club on May 2.

Trackmen Prefer Strange Cinders for Conquests

Unlike some of our other teams in the past winter and current spring season, Coach Morris Kanaly's track and field performers are able to win on alien tracks but lose out at home. Of course the season is comparatively young in this sport as yet but that has been the order to date. Haverford came to South Mountain for the opening meet and captured the laurels by a 78 to 48 score. The Red and Black clad athletes managed to smash a couple of local records in the course of the afternoon so the calibre of their team is not to be considered lightly. Bob Many, basketball and football star, was the only Lehigh man to break the cord on the track when he breezed in an easy winner in the quarter mile. Two of our sophomore field event men, Friedrich in the high jump and Shay in the javelin, were the other first place winners for the hosts.

With only a few days in the interim, the team went over to Muhlenberg and romped away with an easy victory, 92 to 34. Record smashing seemed to be the order of the day, when five dual meet marks were shattered, three by Lehigh men.

The team went down to the Penn Relays and made the best showing in years even though they did place second to N. Y. U. In doing so they defeated the quartets representing Lafayette, Rutgers, Bucknell, Swarthmore, Union and Johns-Hopkins. It is no disgrace to be beaten by N. Y. U. since the Violet now boasts of one of the strongest track teams in the country. So much so that they are resigning from the Middle Atlantic Association to concentrate their efforts in the I. C. A. A. A. A. Three of the four men who composed the quartet are sophomores, leaving Many as the only upper classman.

Circling about to score the winning goal against Penn

Netmen Silence Majority of Opposing Racquet Wielders

After getting off to a late start. Prof. Neil Carothers' tennis team concentrated its action and played three matches in four days, beating Lafayette 8-1, and Washington and Lee, 6-1 handily but losing to Penn 2-7.

Lehigh came mighty close to whitewashing the Maroon in the opening match. Captain Wally Usher of the Brown and White lost in close sets to Lombard, 7-5 and 10-8, which accounted for their only point. Paired with Seligson in the doubles, they had little trouble in downing the Eastonians in straight sets. Seligson and Epstein garnered the two points against Penn, both winning their singles matches. Seligson was feeling very poorly on the day of this meet so did not compete in the doubles. This gave Penn a clean sweep in this division but only after some rather prolonged struggles, one set going to 14-12 and another to 13-11.

Lacrosse Team Strikes Snags on Foreign Fields

The lacrosse team got all keyed up at house party time and sent Penn back to Philadelphia with a 4 to 3 defeat. In this game the team looked like an old time Brown and White aggregation in this sport and it even appeared possible

that Lehigh was due to regain some of its lost prestige in the old Indian game. Penn has its best team in years and held Johns-Hopkins to four goals. Whether this success went to the heads of our team or just what is the matter is not definitely known but the fact remains that the next two games were lost to Princeton and Rutgers, neither of whom is especially good this year.

The season opened with the usual defeat of Lafayette followed by a defeat by the Navy (which might also be classed as "usual" since we have not defeated the Midshipmen in several years). The team is an enigma to its closest followers. There are good attack men and the defense has proved almost impenetrable at times only to appear equally as weak on other occasions. We do have a sophomore goal tender, Werft, who is the equal of any who has worn the Brown and White in several years. If this team can strike its stride there is no reason why it should suffer any more defeats.

The schedule:

		Opp.	L.U.
April 10	Lafayette	3	5
April 13	Navy	11	1
April 20	Penn	3	4
April 24	Princeton	5	1
April 27	Rutgers	5	2
May 4	Stevens	Home	
May 11	Swarthmore	Away	
May 18	Montclair A. C.	Home	

View of Library from Drown Hall showing relative size of old and new

Detroit Club Entertains Prospective Students

About twenty-five members of the Detroit Club turned out at the University Club on the evening of April 19 for a delightful dinner and gab-fest to which several Detroit boys who are contemplating college next Fall had been invited. The youngsters certainly got an earful about the glories of Lehigh, not only from the official academic viewpoint but also about "extra-curricular" attractions from Charlie Rennigs to Mealy's. At the speakers' table were President Hutchinson, '02, John Hegeman, '02, Bob Drummond, '06, and Alumni Secretary Buchanan. Buck gave an outline of the things Lehigh offers to the right kind of student, touching both on the scholastic side and on athletics and other activities. Hegeman and Drummond, "unaccustomed" as they are to public speaking, each did a little turn which pleased the crowd. The high spot of the evening's entertainment was the projection of three reels of Lehigh movies which brought back many a fond memory and gave an insight into the remarkable growth and progress at the University in the past few years.

The Detroit Club is quite set up over the fact that the nominees for President and Vice-President of the Alumni Association for next year are both members of the club. They are A. R. Glancy, '03, and E. F. Johnson, '07. Members of the club hope to carry out a program of activity next year that will establish the motor city as an important center of Lehigh influence.

Washington Club Elects New Officers

The annual spring meeting of the Washington Lehigh Club was held in the Cosmos Club on April 11. The guest of the evening was Alumni Secretary Buchanan who recounted current events of interest on the campus and discussed a number of questions brought up by members of the club. The highlight of the evening was the showing of three reels of Lehigh movies which were greatly enjoyed, particularly by a number of men who have not been able to visit the campus recently.

New officers were elected in the course of the evening as follows: President, T. N. Gill, '07, Secretary, C. B. Griffith, '28. The new administration is planning more frequent meetings for next year and is anxious to add to the club's mailing list the names of many Lehigh men who have located in the capital recently and have not

been receiving notices of the meetings. Another activity that is already under way, is intended to increase the quota of Lehigh news in the Washington papers. The officers of the Club have made contact with some of the local newspapermen and will see that the regular press releases sent out from the University receive sympathetic consideration by the editors.

Those present at the meeting were: F. S. Borden, '11, H. J. Phillips, '18, R. B. Swope, '10, W. W. Hoeke, '28, C. B. Griffith, '28, J. F. Nolan, '21, C. W. Mitman, '09, Dr. W. F. Burdick, '24, N. H. Heck, '03, G. Y. Custer, '18, S. Scrivener, Jr., '27, W. Y. Brady, '92, A. E. Phillips, '90, E. R. Greenleaf, '20, C. R. Whyte, '12, S. K. Hoagland, '17, D. M. Wight, '23, J. A. Watson, '84, T. N. Gill, '07, H. Shepherd, '18, H. S. Jacoby, '77, C. C. Ailes, '12, and J. H. Olcott, '23.

Baltimore Club Holds Sub-Freshman Party

IT RAINED great guns in Baltimore on the evening of April 9 but no one ever stayed away from a Lehigh party because it was wet. The University Club was the scene of a highly successful spring meeting of the Maryland Lehigh Club at which the local alumni were hosts to a promising crowd of prospective college men. The event was the culmination of plans by Jack Rowan, '10, President of the Club, to increase the quota of Maryland boys in the Lehigh student body. It was pleasant to notice several Lehigh sons among the Sub-Freshmen, including a young Rowan and a young Kutzleb.

Frank Roberts, '02, lead off the speaking program with a short talk on what his Lehigh training has meant to him in his business career. Next, Dean McConn talked about the academic side of Lehigh life and explained

just what kind of an education a student may expect to get at Lehigh. The Dean has the happy knack of making almost as interesting a narrative out of such a subject as S. S. Van Dine makes out of a couple of corpses. He was talking to the Sub-Freshmen but there were a lot of Lehigh graduates present who got almost as much education as the kids.

Alumni Secretary Buchanan told the boys what distinguished company they might expect to enter when they were graduated from Lehigh, outlining the many notable achievements of Lehigh alumni. Finally, Walter R. Okeson topped off the formal program with one of his typically inspiring speeches about Lehigh life and the phases of it that most appeal to boys.

Toward the shank of the evening a buffet supper was enthusiastically assimilated by everybody.

Northeastern Pennsylvania Club Has Gala Night

A crowd of over 70 "singin' fools" who not only sang but yelled and kidded with typical Lehigh enthusiasm, taxed the facilities of the Scranton Club on April 24, the occasion of the annual spring meeting of the N.E. Pennsylvania Lehigh Club. All the regulars from miles around were out in force. The roll-call of the meeting would have sounded like a blue book of the anthracite industry of Pennsylvania. An exceptionally fine program may have accounted for some of the unusually large turn-out, but the only explanation of the high pitch of enthusiasm and pep was that everybody just felt like having a good time.

The principal speaker of the evening was the well-known geologist, Dr. Henry M. Payne, of Washington, D. C., of the American Mining Congress. Dr. Paine has attained world wide recognition in the geological field, having

Speakers' Table at Northeastern Pennsylvania Club's Dinner
E. T. Conner, A. C. Dodson, H. M. Payne, H. A. Butler, G. H. Bingham,
N. M. Emery, C. Evans

served on several government commissions for the exploitation of natural resources, spent considerable time in the Arctic in the development of gold dredges and served as consulting engineer to the Imperial Russian Government.

Dr. Paine spoke on the history of the many spectacular booms that stand out as romantic highlights of industrial history, from the South Sea Bubble in England in 1711 through the Mississippi Bubble and down to the Florida boom of 1925. He contrasted the mushroom growth of such flurries with the substantial progress that results from the vision of men trained in industrial leadership and emphasized the need of America for well-balanced industrial leaders.

H. A. Butler, '83, of Mauch Chunk, was drafted by the Club as toastmaster for the evening and he entered a strong bid for the Lehigh championship in the art. Butler has an uncanny knack of quieting an audience which is rocking with laughter by leading it off in a solemn, serious vein, only to send it off into new convulsions by his droll witticisms. Every time there was a chance to get in a word edgeways, the crowd called for his famous discourse on "Mules" and finally he had to accede with some of the anecdotes about that much abused species.

Dr. N. M. Emery, Vice-President of the University, spoke of some of the changes that have taken place on the campus in the last few years, including additions to the physical plant and changes in the various curricula. Eli T. Conner, prominent consulting engineer of Scranton, was called on for a few words and responded with a plea for more imagination on the part of engineers, saying that vision was the most important faculty that a technical man could possess. Alan C. Dodson, President of the Weston Dodson Coal Company of Bethlehem, and one of Lehigh's trustees, was present and responded to a toast with a few well chosen remarks.

In addition to the singing of Lehigh songs and popular favorites by the crowd, the musical program was topped off by some splendid baritone solos rendered by Mr. J. A. Gilbert of Mauch Chunk, who accompanied Toastmaster Butler to the meeting. The new Lehigh movies were projected, much to the satisfaction of the crowd, although Buck turned out to be a "ham" as operator of the machine. It was midnight before the Alma Mater wound up the evening's jollification.

B. E. Schaeffer, '22, was elected president of the Club for 1929-30. Other officers named to serve for the ensuing year were: E. J. Garra, '25, vice-president; G. H. Bingham, '10, secretary-treasurer; E. Schweitzer, '07, assistant secretary-treasurer; G. R. Wood, '11, G. E. Shepherd, '94, J. H. Hart, '12, and E. H. Lawall, '82, members of the executive committee.

Rout of Army in 11-inning Skirmish Brings Team Fourth Victory in Five Games this Season

THE BASEBALL team has reached the middle of its season with a percentage of .800, having won four out of the five games played to date. Four other contests were washed off the schedule by rain. The latest and outstanding conquest by this team was a hectic eleven inning battle in which the Army nine was beaten, 6 to 5. It was one of those ball games that appear more often in fiction than reality where the home team comes through in the pinch and wins out. Incidentally, the Cadets are coached by "Moose" McCormick, '04, and this game had been one of his principal objectives all season. It is even claimed that he deliberately took his best pitcher out of a game with Lafayette three days before his game with Lehigh in order to save him for us. The Army was leading Lafayette at the time but lost that game as well as ours as a result of this change in pitchers.

The Army started off the game by scoring a run but Lehigh tied it, or rather Bob Harris, our first baseman, tied it personally by a home run over the right field wall. This was his first of five consecutive hits and what was intended to be a sacrifice fly on his sixth trip to the plate. He is the same young man that hurled the successful forwards against Lafayette last November. The visitors picked up two more runs up to the eighth inning and then we again tied it up when Wint. Miller, who was playing his second full game as an outfielder, duplicated Harris' feat and

clouted Lehigh's second homer. Harris was on base at the time as a result of his fourth safe hit. The ninth was scoreless, but things looked bad in the tenth when Humber of the Cadets broke into the home run column and was preceded across the plate by a team mate. A lot of people including the Army thought the game was just about over. In fact the visitors even packed their bats away but Lehigh was far from licked. Bennett and Harris singled and were sacrificed by Miller. Then Jones came through with a single and the count was again knotted. Strauss, who had borne the pitching burden for the entire eleven innings scored the winning run after the bases were loaded and Harris hit a short fly to left which was dropped by the fielder and the catcher on the throw home.

The only other games played since the last BULLETIN were with Princeton and Haverford. The former constitutes the only loss to date and the bitter part of it from the Lehigh standpoint is that it was lost for no good reason at all. It was a poorly played game regardless of which team you favored but apparently Lehigh played a trifle poorer than the Tigers. The Brown and White did out-hit the Tigers, 8 to 5, but did not make as good use of the safe blows, enabling the home team to win 4 to 3.

Haverford was blanked 7 to 0. Harry Hesse, our basketball captain, held the Main Liners to five safe hits while our batters collected fourteen.

The schedule:

ALUMNI DAY
JUNE 8
A SURE CURE FOR WHAT AILS YOU

		Opp.	L.U.
April 2	Villanova	8	10
April 3	Drexel	0	8
April 10	Temple ....Rain		
April 13	Princeton	4	3
April 20	Rutgers ....Rain		
April 24	Haverford	0	7
April 27	Army ....(11 ins.)	5	6
May 1	Muhlenberg	6	8
May 4	Lafayette ....Away		
May 7	Penn ....Away		
May 8	C. C. N. Y........Home		
May 11	Lafayette ....Home		
May 15	Rutgers ....Home		
May 18	Lafayette ....Away		
June 7	Muhlenberg ......Home		
June 8	Villanova ....Home		

"Dear Dad"

Letters of a Lehigh Junior and His Lehigh Father

Dear Dad:

Well, I guess you think I must have passed out or something but I just simply haven't had a chance to write. Things have been happening so fast around here that every minute is precious. When a man gets loaded up with so many responsibilities he simply has to make every second count. Like tonight, for instance, I had to go to Pi Delta Epsilon initiation—that's the national honorary journalistic fraternity and we take in the fellows who have made good in publication work and try to raise the standards of college journalism and lead student thought in the right direction. Well, here I was just initiated and the fellows insisted on electing me second vice-president and of course, a fellow has to take his share of these responsibilities, even if his time is pretty valuable.

Well, by the time I got back to the house it was almost midnight and when I came in I found a bunch of the frosh in a bull session in Skrimy Jackson's room. When the fellows elected me head of the house I told them that from then on there would be no more bull sessions because these kids came to college to learn something and not sit around arguing a lot of hot air, so I told them to bust up the session. I let them see right from the start that I mean what I say so they didn't give me any argument. It turned out they were arguing about whether a guy ought to get married young or save his money and it took me until 1:30 to convince that sap Humpy that he was all wet. Well, anyway, I'll get some discipline around the house and that's what they need, with the freshmen getting away with murder and chewing gum in chapter meeting and not addressing the chair properly and things like that.

Well, that's the way it is every night lately, and I'm just snatching a few minutes about 2 a.m. to let you know I'm all right and with the end of the month and everything I guess you've been wondering what's the matter. By the way there'll be a house party assessment this month although I didn't have a girl as I couldn't afford to waste the time with so much going on and anyway I figured I better be free to see that

things ran off all right and that the alumni didn't get too tight or the Dean walk in unexpectedly or something. Also need a little extra on account of Sub-Freshman Day. We had 14 kids up for it and had to buy them dinners, etc. It was pretty good, especially the ball game as we beat the Army in 11 innings and their coach was up at the house afterward and he sure was disgusted.

Nothing much new, Dad, except that Jack Petrikin has a new hat which is making a big hit around college. Spring football practice is over. I was out some but couldn't get out every day with the Mustard and Cheese going on and all the other responsibilities I've got loaded on me lately. The show was pretty good. We had it for house party and again for Sub-freshman Day and going to Philly on Thursday. Well, I sure am sleepy and guess I better stop now.

Love from
FRANK.

———

Dear Son:

So you are now engaged in trying "to lead student thought in the right direction." Well, I will give you the same advice Mark Twain, P. T. Barnum or Henry the Eighth (I forget which) gave to the young man about to marry—DON'T! Never waste your time, son, trying to lead anybody's thought in the right direction. In the first place you are quite unlikely to know which direction is right and in the second place trying to make another chap think straight is worse than riding herd on a bunch of milling cattle. You devote any spare energy you have to trying to think straight yourself and that job, even if only half done, will certainly sweat up your undershirt.

Of course, I am delighted to hear you are now head of the house. Naturally discipline will improve greatly but I am a little worried as to whether you won't have to give up your extra-curricular activities to say nothing of such side lines as a purblind faculty continue to exact as pre-requisites to graduation. My calculus is rather cob-webby but my arithmetic is still good and I figure if it takes you two hours to break up a freshman bull session that handling a

sophomore drunk (not to mention an alumnus) will be a big night's work for you, as I think of all your other duties I can see no time for books, yet charming as I find your letters it is the ones I get from the Dean which produce, or will fail to produce, checks. Speaking of the Dean I sure am sorry for that estimable gentleman now that he must cope for a year to come with the master-minds you have hinted to me your class contains. It's a terrible job for an administration when a smart senior class grasps the helm.

Seriously, son, I want you to remember that next year, you, as a Senior, are one of the governing heads of the student body. If you Seniors are worth while chaps who think straight and play square the rest of the college will toddle right along in your footsteps. It's your last year; Make it one you will be proud to remember.

I like that Sub-freshman Day idea. It's fine to have you fellows in the frats entertaining these embryo Lehigh men even if the motive is not entirely free from a trace of selfish forethought. So I am going to send a check and what's more it is a good big one. I think you are really trying to do a job and I'll gamble a few blue chips on you. Of course if you slip in your exams there's a tough summer ahead of you. From now on until you graduate I don't want you to know there is any such animal as a Dean at Lehigh. I want him to hear so little about you that he will give a start of surprise when he reads your name on your diploma in June, 1930. Don't you worry about him dropping in on the house during a house party. Keep your mind set on avoiding the receipt of any notes requesting you to drop in at his office. I don't care and he don't care if you are so unfamiliar with him that you have trouble recollecting his name. Get busy! Crack those books!!

Yours from Missouri,
DAD.

P.S. My class don't have any reunion this year but I have a big red circle around June 7 and 8 on my Lehigh calendar. I'll expect you home before I leave because I have a good job to start you on this summer.

OBITUARIES

C. Philip Coleman, '88

Charles Philip Coleman, president of the Mount Hope Bridge Company and formerly president of the Worthington Pump and Machinery Corporation, died of pneumonia in Washington on April 13, aged 64 years. He was enroute to the South for a vacation when he became ill on the train and was removed to the Hotel Mayflower, where he died. The bridge company of which he was the controlling officer is constructing a $4,000,000 bridge across Narragansett Bay. Recent tests of the cable work in the bridge indicated that it was inadequate and that it would be necessary to do the work over at a cost of about $750,000. It is believed that this was a contributory cause to his death.

He was a member of many clubs in and around New York City. He was a life member of the Alumni Association and was a member of the Sigma Phi Fraternity. He is survived by his widow and two sons.

W. S. Cope, '90

Warren Scott Cope, a civil engineer in Crumpler, West Virginia, died of diabetes in St. Luke's Hospital, Bluefield, on January 2. He had been suffering from this disease for several years. He was sixty years of age.

Cope had long been identified with the development of southern West Virginia, first going there in the employ of the Norfolk and Western Railroad. He is survived by his widow, his mother, six sons and one sister.

Harold I. Fair, '16

The Rev. Harold I. Fair, rector of St. John's Episcopal Church, Fall River, Mass., died of carbon monoxide poisoning on April 13, at his home there, aged 37 years. He had been in ill health for some time and had just returned from a vacation in New Hampshire.

Fair was a World War veteran with a distinguished record, having been wounded in action as well as gassed and shell shocked. He had been a captain in the 101st Infantry, Yankee Division, and had been awarded the distinguished service cross for bravery at Belleau Bois, north of Verdun. After his graduation from Lehigh he studied at Oxford and was later graduated from the Cambridge Theological Seminary in 1921.

He is survived by three children, the oldest of whom is seven. He was a member of the Beta Theta Pi Fraternity.

H. E. Dimmick, '19

Harold Edgerton Dimmick, vice-president of the H. B. Potter Company, Plainfield, N. J., died the latter part of 1927. He served as an aviation instructor during the war. He also attended M. I. T. He was a member of the Kappa Alpha fraternity.

PERSONALS

Class of 1889

40-YEAR REUNION, JUNE 8, 1929

C. W. Hudson, Correspondent
15 Park Row, New York City

S. E. Lambert from Pasadena, Cal., writes that he is coming to commencement and the '89 reunion to take in the whole thing from start to finish.

Arch Johnston, president of the class, told me last Monday that he wishes me to say in the BULLETIN that he wants every man in the class to be his guest for dinner on Saturday evening, June 8. To those of us who have on many occasions enjoyed Arch's generous hospitality, I know this renewed invitation for our 40th reunion will mean another evening of carefree comradeship. Let's be sure and enjoy it while we may. Arch also told me that Secretary Cornelius and himself will work out the other details for our reunion so that the class can take part in the commencement exercises. It just occurs to me that *exercises* is the proper name for the Alumni Day events.

Class of 1890

H. A. Foering, Correspondent
828 W. Broad St., Bethlehem, Pa.

George Barclay is Assistant Manager of El Jardin Hotel at Brownsville, Texas. He writes that he was given a couple weeks' vacation and took an airplane jaunt over Mexico, spending some time in the Capital city. He says airplane traveling in Mexico is far safer than the railroads.

H. S. Landis has retired from his editorial duties, and is enjoying his hobby of collecting antiques of various kinds. He has a private museum of his own. According to Neumeyer, who called upon him there and looked it over, it must contain, at a moderate estimate, $100,000 worth of valuable, choice antiques.

I have just had a letter from Cullum, who has been in Europe for some time and is now at the Californie Palace in Cannes, France.

Class of 1891

Walton Forstall, Correspondent
Broad and Arch Sts., Philadelphia, Pa.

I think someone once said that there were compensations in all things. This class agent is finding out the truth of this saying. A small class is jake when it comes to writing letters asking for checks to the Alumni Association, but it is all wet when news is needed for this column every month. Talk about making bricks without straw. That is an easy job; something like taking candy from children, compared with the task of meeting the demand of the BULLETIN for news each month of a class whose modesty is as great as its numbers are small. This month the news, as Dutchy Ringer used to say, is "seemly zero."

Class of 1894

35-YEAR REUNION, JUNE 8, 1929

Aubrey Weymouth, Correspondent
101 Park Ave., New York City

In the absence of any class news for this issue, the space is being used to remind all '94 men of the 35th year reunion of the class on Alumni Day, Saturday, June 8. You are urged to write to Beinhower at Rutland Vt., as soon as possible and promise him to be back.

Class of 1895

C. F. Townsend, Correspondent
405 Temple St., New Haven, Conn.

H. T. Rights has been appointed bridge engineer of the Lehigh Valley Railroad Co. He was formerly assistant bridge engineer.

It is possible that some of the readers of these notes might know of the address or whereabouts of some of our missing members, and I should appreciate the favor of receiving information regarding any of our men of the following list: S. O. Alcott, W. W. Bending, W. A. Caldwell, Jr., E. B. Clark, N. F. Clark, J. N. Dezendorf, F. M. Fletcher, A. G. Galan, F. Garcia, A. M. Hay, E. E. Holeman, S. G. Jenks, G. A. Lowe, W. McQueen, Jr., W. A. Merritt, H. R. de Oliveira, P. Powers, H. C. Ridgely, P. Rios, A. M. Ros, H. S. Sizer, G. B. VanBrunt, A. Villareal, W. O. Wade, G. P. Wager, H. L. Wood, R. D. Wooldridge, C. Yglesias.

Class of 1896

W. S. Ayars, Correspondent
410 Eng. Bldg., Broadway at 117th St., New York City

From Tommie Gannon comes a long and interesting letter, but Tommie was writing rather more to me than he was to the class, and was blessedly frank. He had quite a bit to say, very pungently, about the wet-and-dry situation, and enclosed a clipping from the *Times* of Dec. 20, about the row raised when Mrs. William Lancaster, wife of a famous British aviator then in the United States, arrived at our hospitable shores with a special aviation compass of the floating variety, containing four ounces of pure alcohol. The conscientious guardians of our national purity were all for draining out the vicious fluid, thereby ruining the instrument, and it took Captain Lancaster many hours of interviewing officials and untangling red tape before the compass could finally be brought ashore. It would seem that the addition of four ounces of pure alcohol to the supply already distributed around the nation would not seriously upset the balance, but the vigilant minions of the 18th Amendment were not going to take any chances. Tommie confesses to having given up baseball as a participant, and says he is not old enough for golf. So he is keeping fit by bowling, and modestly admits to being able "to chalk up 200 now and then"—whatever that means. He bewails Lehigh's failure to beat Lafayette, as usual, but adds that he never misses going to the games. He is still with the Worthington Pump people, working at Harrison, N. J. I thought I did considerable commuting; but living in Brooklyn and working in Harrison beats me completely.

Chester Richmond writes from Chattanooga, Tennessee, where he says he is "selling the earth," as a profession. He mentions that for the benefit of all sufferers, he has discovered a famous and infallible remedy for "flu" in "Tennessee sunshine (not 'moonshine'), and if taken in regular doses of about three fingers every hour, it will either knock it out, or else put the patient where he don't care!" He does not, however, indicate in any manner where this valuable specific may be obtained. He also denies the grandfather honors to Sam Senior: "I have been a grandfather for five years, and that ought to put me pretty well up on the list for '96. I have two husky grandsons whom I hope may be eligible for Lehigh in about the class of 1944." He ends with true southern hospitality: "There are eight or ten Lehigh men living here in Chattanooga and I can assure any of the old bunch a hearty welcome should they drop off in Chattanooga. Try it yourself and see." This may make a strong appeal to chronic sufferers from flu.

Class of 1897

J. H. Pennington, Correspondent
McFarland Foundry and Machine Co.,
Trenton, N. J.

The bald spot below shows you birds how this column looks when you refuse to tell us anything about yourselves for the edification of an anxious world.

Aren't you ashamed?

Class of 1898

H. C. Paddock, Correspondent
Turner Construction Co.,
420 Lexington Ave., New York City

Cy Roper is secretary and treasurer of the Industrial Furnace Corp., 502 Liberty Bank Bldg., Buffalo, N. Y. He is engaged in a kind of engineering business, having applied a special type of electric furnace to the malleableizing of white iron castings, or, in other words, annealing malleable iron. The old process required from 8 to 10 days, the new requires only 3 days, saving 40 to 60 per cent in cost, and giving a product much better and more uniform in physical properties. Annealing is done in the open without the formation of any scale. Cy has patented the process. We wish

him a large measure of success in the venture.

S. B. Merrill is president and general manager of the E. W. Vanduzen Co., Cincinnati, Ohio, founders of church bells. If present research work comes to a reasonable fruition, his firm, he believes, will be the best known in his line. Merrill is also secretary and treasurer of the Cincinnati chapter of the Sigma Nu Alumni, and a member of the Cincinnati Lehigh Alumni.

Class of 1899

30-YEAR REUNION, JUNE 8, 1929
Arthur W. Klein, Correspondent
43 Wall St., Bethlehem, Pa.

E. G. Grace has returned from Aiken, S. C., where he spent some time resting and playing golf. He is again actively engaged in directing the operation and shaping the policies of Bethlehem Steel.

P. G. L. Hilken has recently returned from a trip to South America. His address is 135 W. 71st St., New York City.

H. E. Knight is a colonel in the United States Army. He is stationed at present at The Infantry School, Fort Benning, Ga.

Assurances of attendance at the 30-year Reunion in June are pouring in from various members of the Class and it begins to look as if the number coming back will break all previous '99 records.

Class of 1900

Edward A. Yellis, Correspondent
405 W. Broad St., Bethlehem, Pa.

W. T. McCarthy, our Mac, just evolved an idea as a solution of the traffic conjestion along Fulton Street, Brooklyn. He suggests that sidewalks in the busy shopping section be balconies two stories above the present street level. Mac says:

Your letter of March 9 has been troubling my conscience, so, as this is the first opportunity I have had, in the midst of a number of activities, I am going to clean my slate.

The first thing I always look for is news of 1900, but most often I am disappointed. It always was a modest bunch and I rarely see any of its members. However, a short time ago, friend wife and I went into a restaurant in Flatbush and saw a lady we knew seated at another table with a big fellow whose back was towards us, and who was not her husband. She smiled and nodded and in a few minutes, to see whom she was speaking to I suppose, Andy Brice's face appeared around the corner. The big fellow was his son and the lady his wife. I'll bet that Andy, with all his old ability as a boxer, has to watch his step.

Fred Groff is here in Brooklyn with the B. M. T. helping to keep the subway cars running for the daily millions. His son is also big enough to put it all over dad. This condition seems to be so almost uniVersal that I sometimes wonder just what influence Lehigh had.

As for myself, there is very little to tell—most of the time, however, plugging along on plans, and trying to learn how to become an expert collector; but have about concluded after all these years that I can never develop much ability in that direction.

Hope your letter may have stirred up some more of the gang.

Class of 1901

E. T. Murphy, Correspondent
Carrier Eng. Corp.,
850 Frelinghuysen Ave., Newark, N. J.

I got this most interesting letter from John Rittenhouse who wrote from Baleares, Spain:

Your S.O.S. of Feb. 7 has just completed a circuitous voyage of about eleven thousand miles, and, as a reward for its persistence, will be given temporary precedence over the story of my own wanderings, which I am now preparing for publication.

This delightful little island which so few people have ever heard of, is an ideal refuge from the climatic inclemencies of the continent. Here one can be gay or quiet, play or

work, and rest up after, and in preparation for, the strain of constant travel.

Just a year ago I was in Colombo and most of the other interesting places of Ceylon. Prior to that, for several months the Hawaiian and Philippine Islands, Japan, China, the Malay peninsula and a few out of the way places—afterward Egypt, Italy, Switzerland, Austria, Hungary, Czecho Slovakia, Germany, Belgium, France, Algeria. Many of these places I knew, others were unfamiliar—all are different, not only from America, but from each other. The functions of government, the habits and customs of the people, the religions, the economic life, the scenery and climate, the political tendencies—each country is a study in itself, and forms some kind of a basis of comparison for the stage of civilization and progress our own country has attained.

If a man expects an American breakfast, American comforts, American habits of thought, let him stay in America—if he is willing and able to adapt himself to the customs and general scheme of things in the various places he visits, he will learn many things, and consciously or unconsciously absorb something of the beauty and artistry and culture of his surroundings.

But you can't fight and argue—otherwise the Pyramids and the Coliseum will remain a mental picture or blurred as if you'd photographed them both on the same plate.

From here I am returning to Algeria; motoring through the Northern Sahara, then France, England, the Scandanavian country and New York in the fall, at which time I will drop in on you and have you buy my lunch as I'll probably be looking for hand-outs.

With kindest regards to all my old classmates and other Lehigh men.

Class of 1903

S. P. Felix, Correspondent
Schaff Building, 15th and Race Sts.,
Philadelphia, Pa.

The postcard idea is working splendidly. More news is available than the next two issues can hold.

George Goodwin has written in detail of his 9,000-mile tour of the States from which we cull the following: In San Antonio after I had chatted with a young bricklayer for a couple of hours he volunteered the information that he was nineteen and it occurred to me to find out what ravages three weeks of travel had made in my appearance, so I asked him to guess my age. On due consideration he replied, "thirty or thirty-two." Now this reminded me of Bobby Heck; for once upon a time the problem of my life was to convince Bobby that I was over seven. I believe Bobby suspected me of being the culprit who erased the chalk mark on the first tooth counted on that big gear the day Bobby counted around two or three times before he discovered the deception. But no one could accuse me of being the genius who said, "We fellows who know all about this part of the subject can go home now, can't we, Professor?" It took Droll to say that.

Snyder Radio Shop, Riverside, Cal., says, "Hello Sam, Old Timer, as long as you invested in this card, thought I'd better return it to you! Twelve years out here has almost made me a native son. Kindest regards to all the boys." Oran C. Snyder is proprietor.

Charlie Young is department commander of Sons of Union Veterans of the Civil War, State of Pennsylvania.

Art Frick reminds us the trout season opened on the 15th, and says that he heard Pop Wolcott's radio show the other night and it was too much for him. He further states, "Eldest daughter Mary Norris, is engaged to a Harvard, '26 man, so you see what the football game did last fall. Jack on crew at Asheville School — wife still bossing women of the state so I'm just "goin' fishin'!" This is good copy, Art, come again.

Planning high-speed business

An Advertisement of the
American Telephone and Telegraph Company

MORE than 95% of the telephone calls from one town to another in the Bell System are now on a high-speed basis. This holds whether the call is from New Orleans to Boston or from New York to Oyster Bay.

Even if it is a long call, the operator in many cases now asks you to hold the telephone while the call is put through.

Calls from one town to another used to be handled by one operator taking your order and giving it to another group of operators to put through. You now give your call direct to the operators who put it through —and put it through fast while you are on.

the line. The average time for handling all toll and long distance calls in the Bell System was further materially reduced in 1928.

A high-speed service to all parts of the country—calls from one town to another as swift, clear and easy as local calls—that is the aim of the Bell System.

This is one of the many improvements in methods and appliances which are constantly being introduced to give high-speed telephone service.

Better and better telephone service at the lowest cost is ever the goal of the Bell System.

"THE TELEPHONE BOOKS ARE THE DIRECTORY OF THE NATION"

Hop Watters is sitting up nights nowadays. A 1500 ton lift span for the Pennsylvania-Newark bay bridge, as a result of the high wind April 1 has to be taken out of the bay and jacked up 50 feet. Anyone trying April fool jokes on Hop in the future will get a cold reception.

C. J. Hendrickson is engineer with the Bell Telephone Laboratories, 463 West St., New York.

Nick Heck has recently gotten out a new publication *Earthquakes in the United States*. Can you imagine Nick flirting with this kind of dynamite?

Leslie Wolcott, '25, Pop's son, took an engineering course at Lehigh and a master's degree in Business Administration and Finance at Harvard two years later. He finished at twenty-three years of age, was an honor student all the way through, and made Tau Beta Pi. He showed the old man up a little, but then he didn't have to put in quite so many hours helping to work his way through school. Our money is still on Pop!

This is the kind of news we like to receive. What our sons and daughters are doing is of real human interest.

Class of 1904

25-YEAR REUNION, JUNE 8, 1929
F. P. Sinn, Correspondent
160 Front St., New York City

Jesse Underwood says that he will be at the reunion unless his old body fails him entirely. Jesse left Wall Street in the early part of 1917 to enter the war. He drew the Second Division and accumulated some French and a lot of bad health. Upon his return to this country he spent a long time in the Walter Reed Hospital, in Washington, D. C., and since his discharge, nearly ten years ago, has been seeking health. In closing he says, "Have no job, but am laughing my way through life, so far so good."

May the next ten years be a better ten for you, Jesse.

John McCleary writes:

Knowing that the committee on arrangements will not look kindly on last minute surprises, I hasten to throw my hat in the ring and you may put in my order for an umbrella. This is not a sudden impulse as I have had such a step in mind for 25 years, so am eagerly looking forward to being with the old gang again. No doubt a few of us, on account of having become disfigured with bald knobs and gray locks, may have some difficulty in identifying ourselves—but I am willing to take a chance.

As for news about myself—this is, of necessity, very brief. Up until 1908 I was a believer in the story of the rolling stone and tried to establish a new record. Since then I have been with my present company—the last 3 years at the home office. This is the first time that the occasion of a reunion has found me sufficiently near to Bethlehem to feel reasonably certain of being able to be on hand. I second Kirk Johnson's efforts to depart from the seriousness of the occasion—which I know will be a great relief to Don Packer.

W. M. Lalor and the W. M. Lalor Co. have moved to 20 E. Jackson Blvd., Chicago, Ill.

W. R. Shively has left Brooklyn for 85 Halsted St., East Orange, N. J.

Class of 1905

W. H. Lesser, Correspondent
Third and Frack Sts., Frackville, Pa.

Paul Butler, whose address was lost, has been found. He is sales manager for H. Hammarquist, general contractor and real estate, 349 E. 75th St., Chicago, Ill. Paul lives at 3008 E. 78th St., Chicago.

Bill Larkin is managing the shop of Larkin and Co., makers of drilling tools. Bill's shop is located at Butler, Pa., which is near Pittsburgh. An airport is being built at Butler, and all 1905 fliers are invited to stop off and see him.

The following was clipped from the Washington, D. C., *Evening Star*: "Capt. Hugh P. Oram, Corps of Engineers, attached to the Engineers' School at Fort Humphreys, Va., was ordered to Washington for duty as assistant to Colonel William B. Ladue, Engineer Commissioner of the District. One of the important recent assignments of Capt. Oram was that one which detailed him to duty at Florence, Ala., in connection with the construction of the great Wilson Dam of the Muscle Shoals power project." I am sure that the members of the class will be pleased to hear of the honors merited by Capt. Oram.

This letter was received from Dick Roszel and it is so good that it is printed as received:

There is nothing in the BULLETIN that has quite as much interest for me as the notes about 1905, and it seems to me that the older I get the more pleasure it gives me to see or hear something about the old gang. I often think how fine it would be to turn back a heap of years, gather a whole lot of the '05 boys around the tables in the old Brighton, steins full, and then talk fest as per our sophomore days, but Father Time and Mr. Volstead will not allow.

I have wandered around since 1905, doing some engineering and now I have an automobile business here in Baltimore. We have good racing tracks in Maryland, and I get a big kick out of horse racing. Tight only very seldom! I see very few Lehigh men. Occasionally meet Bob Lyons, Addison Armstrong and Si Deistler, they all look well and prosperous.

Give my best to any and all of the boys when you see them.

Dick's address is Locomobile Co. of Maryland, 913 N. Howard St., Baltimore.

Class of 1908

W. D. Sanderson, Correspondent
706 Liberty Bank Bldg., Buffalo, N. Y.

Jim Fair, local man about town, inventor, railroad man, etc., et. al, has threatened the correspondent with libel suit for publication of these monthly items relating to Jim's favorite speakeasies. In order to avoid such a contingency, the following offsetting statement is made: "Jim Fair is regarded by his superior officers as a very efficient railroad man, whose prospects for advancement are considered excellent."

Long Bill Lytle is in the oil business in Titusville. He has so many youngsters in the public school there that they have elected him president of the school board. It is reported that he is also chief of police and head of the fire department, but we do not vouch for these latter jobs.

Monty Raine was seen around Chicago recently and had apparently fully recovered from the last reunion. He is getting in training for the next.

Another of the lost has been found. F. R. McDonnell's address is % Postmaster, Seattle, Washington.—U. S. S. Juson.

There are eight members of the class still among the missing. We publish the list once more in the hope that the Sherlock Holmes efforts on the part of the balance of the class will uncover their present whereabouts: E. Beato, P. M. Evans, W. E. Frankenfield, H. K. Hartsuff, H. N. Lloyd, R. J. Motz, C. H. Reel, P. L. Semmel.

Skeet Pierce was in Buffalo a short time ago and reported wheat business in western Canada as very good indeed.

Just why he came down here is a mystery. Perhaps it was to compare the beverages here with those to which he is accustomed in that land of the free—lunch.

Mr. and Mrs. A. Oram Fulton have just returned from a delightful six weeks in California. Fulton is still president of the Wheelock, Lovejoy Co., Inc., Cambridge, Mass., and has acquired an enviable position in the business and social life of New England. Even the great have their troubles. A few nights ago a bean-eater in a 1924 Reo carrying no insurance, crashed into Oram's new Cadillac, with considerable damage to the latter, but fortunately inflicting no personal injuries. I would like to reprint what Oram says about him, but alas, the Postal regulations prevent it!

Haldeman Finnie, vice-president and general manager of the Timken-Detroit Co., a subsidiary of the Timken-Detroit Axle Co., manufacturers and distributors of domestic oil burners, was recently elected president of the Oil Heating Institute. We should be inclined to offer congratulations except that experience tells us that these trade association jobs involve plenty of hard work and no pay. Letters of commiseration and flowers should be sent to the unfortunate victim, care of his Detroit office.

A belated explanation of the unsettled conditions in Spain reaches us in the form of news that Nagel has been in that part of the world for the past few months.

John Donegan and Bill Mackie are holding forth with E. L. Phillips & Co., Brooklyn, N. Y. They have been too busy of late to go over to Manhattan Island, but both promise to do this and send in the latest news for the next issue of the BULLETIN.

A. B. Lakey has been appointed walking delegate of the "Benevolent Order of Broadhead Busters." He travels from coast to coast, so nobody need be surprised if they meet him. This is a tip to any of the boys who might want to try something just because they are away from home.

Class of 1909

20-YEAR REUNION, JUNE 8, 1929
D. M. Petty, Correspondent
Beverly and Paul Aves., Bethlehem, Pa.

For the first time, we have caught the Alumni office, as well as the Dean's office, in a mistake. This is how it happened. When we heard from Les Carrier that his son would enter Lehigh next fall, we immediately asked Buck, if there were any sons of '09 men in Lehigh at the present time and the best he could do was to give us the names of 3 nephews. Therefore the arrival of a son of '09 at Lehigh appeared to be a good story and your reporter immediately announced the fact.

As it has turned out, it is a good story for 3 reasons: 1st—Lehigh is where the sons of '09 men should go, 2nd—It enabled your reporter to locate the holder of the '09 cup, 3rd—it established the fact that the holder of the class cup entered Lehigh in the fall of 1928 and, running true to form, the first son of '09 was the first to enter Lehigh. We are glad to announce therefore, that when Les Carrier, Jr., enters Lehigh in the fall of 1929, he will have a loving '09 sophomore to look after him, and, in the true '09 fashion, teach him Lehigh spirit.

If this were a continued story, I, of course, should not divulge the name of the holder of the '09 cup, but refer you to the next issue, but hoping that perhaps the publication of the name of this Lehigh-man will bring forth additional information, I take pleasure in introducing to you the holder of the '09 cup, the first son of an '09 man to enter Lehigh, Raymond K. Serfass, Jr., Lehigh, '32. Ray says, and I can vouch for the fact, that he has not attended many class reunions, but promises to be on hand in June, the Lord willing, and the cup holder will also be on hand.

Al Bellis recently discovered Reds McMurtrie, living in Pittsburgh, East Liberty. Al failed to get the street number. Therefore, if anyone runs across Reds, please send in his mailing address. It certainly would be great to have the old battery, Serfass and McMurtrie, on hand at our 20th reunion.

John Young reports from Charleston, S. C., that he hopes to be on hand in June and that he is living the life of a lazy Southerner and likes it. His address is Berkeley Court, Charleston, S.C.

Tom Coyle reports that while he and Tom Uptegraff have no sons, they are talking about bringing their daughters to Bethlehem next June. This will be fine as I am sure that some of the sons of '09 will be glad to see some of the daughters.

Cope Callen recently addressed the Rock Springs chapter of the Rocky Mts. Mining Institution. Cope was pleading the cause of the young mining engineer, and you know how.

J. Ross N. Corbin is now living at 123 Clinton Ave., New Rochelle, N. Y.

Lloyd C. Taylor is now living at 1603 Park Avenue, Richmond, Va.

Say, boys, the '09 average of those who have given to Lehigh this year is only 2 per cent above the average for the entire Alumni group. I am sure that we are more than a 2 per cent better class. Let's see what can be done about this!

Class of 1910
M. L. Jacobs, Correspondent
837 Tioga Ave., Bethlehem, Pa.

H. J. Zane, Jr., from whom I have not heard in a long time, sends a very welcome card with a lot of good dope. He is living at 519 Springdale Ave., East Orange, N. J. His office is at 225 Broadway, New York City. With another Pennsylvania Dutchman by the name of Hartenstine he conducts the Hartenstine-Zane Co., which specializes in mill buildings, radio towers and hangars. They have been operating since 1916, both having left McClintic-Marshall at that time. Much of their work is in Central and South America which shows their good sense, those countries still having liberty and freedom. Stop in and see us, Zane. We are always glad to hear from you.

Class of 1912
Morton Sultzer, Correspondent
195 Broadway, New York City

Johnny Herr has been on the sick list for two years. Since his case was diagnosed recently as chemical poisoning, he has made fine progress and hopes soon to leave the Union Memorial Hospital in Baltimore where he has been for several months. His headquarters are with

the duPont Co., at Parlin, N. J., where, he says, "We try to make a living for the poor stockholders of this company by making and actually selling Duco." Sounds more like he tried to eat it.

Class of 1913

R. T. Dynan, Correspondent
540 Eighth Ave., Bethlehem, Pa.

J. H. Fogg, whose address was missing, has been located. He lives at 416 N. Maple Ave., Greensburg, Pa.

D. H. Levan, whose address was also lost, is manager of the Savannah Gas Co., P. O. Box 1313, Savannah, Ga. He lives at Gordonston, Savannah, Ga.

E. F. Price lives at 6499 Morris Park Rd., Overbrook, Philadelphia, Pa.

C. R. Streets, another missing man to be located, is vice-president of the Erickson Brick Co., of Bridgeton, N. J. He lives at 283 South Ave., Bridgeton, N. J.

E. C. Wilson, who was in the same boat as Fogg, Levan and Streets, is first vice-president of the National Railway Signal Co., at 1529 Columbus Ave., Boston, Mass. He lives at 8 Lakeville Place, Jamaica Plains, Boston, Mass.

Donald Bowman, who is located at Greenfield, Ind., spent a few days in Bethlehem recently.

Class of 1914

15-YEAR REUNION, JUNE 8, 1929

J. O. Liebig, Correspondent
324 N. 15th Street, Allentown, Pa.

The Big Time is fast drawing nigh. We shall, among other things, convene for a get-together at Spring Valley Inn. You all remember Louie, the genial proprietor. He is ready for us. We have received many suggestions regarding reunion plans, but let us hear from all that wish to add to a successful time. We welcome your opinions NOW. By this time you will no doubt have received cards relative to your attendance. If you have not answered them by this time, do so immediately, and cooperate in making the 1914 reunion a dandy.

C. D. Bickley is living at Greenbrook Acres, North Caldwell, N. J.

W. C. Brooke is structural engineer with the Electric Bond and Share Co., at 2 Rector St., New York City. He lives at 105 Lincoln Park, Newark, N. J.

Percy Sanderson, who was lost to our class, as far as address was concerned, is living temporarily at 229 N. Goundry St., Tonawanda, N. Y.

L. Thornburgh can now be reached at the Navy Yard, Mare Island, Cal.

Here is the very welcome letter I received from Luis Lacombe:

Caixa Postal 114,
Bello Horizonte,
Minas Geraes, Brazil.

Dear Leibig:

It has been a long time since I have met or heard from any old Lehigh man, and your Christmas card sure was a pleasant surprise.

You ask me to give some personal information for the BULLETIN. But first of all, I would like to know just what the BULLETIN is. I have never received or seen a copy of it, and would appreciate your sending me a copy of the last issue. It would feel good to get an inkling of what some of the old boys are doing.

I will try to give you a short account of just what I am doing, and you can use it as you see fit.

Returning to Brazil in May, 1924, I worked for one year with the Atlantic Refining Co., as assistant to their construction engineer. Leaving them in 1925, I entered the General Electric S. A., which is the Brazilian company affiliated with the International General Electric Co., Inc., of Schenectady, and, of course, connected with the General Electric Co. of the U. S. A. First I worked as engineer salesman, but many changes have occurred, and at present I am the manager of the Minas Geraes district office of our company in Brazil, located at the city of Bello Horizonte, Minas Geraes, Brazil. This is our third largest district office, serving a territory inhabited by over 7,000,000 people.

Hope everything is O K with you and that the boys have been giving Lafayette some good beatings. The papers here once in a while give football and baseball results of some of the American universities, but I have lost all track of the Lehigh-Lafayette games.

Art Ward received the following letter from Sanchez.

Business down here is rotten. I'm still in the cattle business and live at Nuevitas, a quiet little town near my ranch. If you ever come to Havana which is quite a town, be sure and let me know so you can come and visit us, and I'll take you out to the finca and let you throw the bull around.

Say, what's the matter with Lehigh in athletics? I suppose they are waiting for A. R. Sanches, Jr., to go up in 1950 and beat Lafayette.

Be sure and let me hear from you again and remember me to all the boys you see. My address now is Gomez 19, Nuevitas, Cuba.

We learn that Joe Parks is manager of the industrial division of the entire middle Atlantic district of the Westinghouse Electric Co., and located in Philadelphia, Pa.

Class of 1916

E. J. Clement, Correspondent
335 Lowell Ave., Floral Park, N. Y.

This job has its high spots. Here are a couple of items that are too good to keep. So as not to betray any confidences they bear the signature of "Lonely Hearts," or what have you.

"Just received a copy of the LEHIGH BULLETIN last night and note that you are the correspondent for 1916. Well, I was one of those things myself about a year ago without intending to be. I was going to be shot (which I'm not as yet) but I hope you do not have such bad luck with your corresponding."

Shades of 1916, here's another: "Part of my duties consist of signing up the girls, so I get all the addresses and 'phone numbers, and if I don't get tripped up by at least one of the 150 odd that we use, it won't be their faults."

C. A. Hiss is transmission engineer of the southern division of the New Jersey Bell Telephone Co. at 28 W. State St., Trenton, N. J. Charlie lives at 725 N. Pennsylvania Ave., Morrisville, Pa.

Class of 1919

A REAL PARTY FOR '19 MEN THIS JUNE.
J. W. Gardiner, Jr., Correspondent
% John T. Lewis and Bros. Co.,
Widener Bldg., Philadelphia, Pa.

The returns that have come in thus far indicate that there will be many more than 19 '19 men on hand. In fact, I believe we can all rejoice in the fact that Buckie MacDonald has accepted and is already functioning as chairman of the Banquet and Parade Committee. Those associated with him on this Committee are: Ken Bevier, Tom Bray, Roy Coffin, Joe Gardiner, Gordon Gildersleeve, Neil Kennedy, Mickie Kirk, Milt Manley, Reds Nawrath, Joe Rosenmiller, Otto Spillman, and Bill Whigham.

In addition to those on the committee, we have already heard from a number of others who are enthusiastic.

It is rather interesting to hear from Ken Bevier that he attended the intercollegiate wrestling matches, showing that he has not forgotten most of his scholastic activities. It is also pleasing to know that he is getting in touch with a number of the class personally,

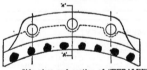

which after all is one of the best means of getting a real turnout.

Bill Winterhalter sends us the following terse information: "Looks as though I'll be there—about children, just have two boys and they hit from both sides of the plate." Knowing Bill as we do we believe he has said a lot.

J. B. Heilman writes from 1703 Jenny Lind St,. McKeesport, Pa., that he is planning to come back for the reunion with the help of God and a few marines, if necessary.

Fred Hazletine, whom we remember was our freshman class treasurer, writes from Portland, Ore., that after knocking around the United States from New England to Florida, Cuba to Panama and now at Oregon, he has always kept in touch with Lehigh news. He plans to come back to this part of the country to live and will be among us this June.

Alphabet Duck writes that he is a 19½ single man, is still happy, and hopes to be more so this June.

The corresponding secretary wishes to say that it has been a real inspiration to serve in that capacity, particularly when the cards and letters come in from various members of the Class all over the world. One has just been received from H. Tsai volunteering the following information.

"I have been in the silk manufacturing business for 8 years and am getting along fairly well. Married and have three children. Hope to hear from my old friends. My address is: % Mayar Silk Mills, Siccawai Road, Shanghai, China."

Class of 1921

A. T. Wilson, Correspondent
1118 W. Market St., Bethlehem, Pa.

Friends, rummies, and class-mates, or what have you—. To say this job was wished on me would not be quite accurate, yet such is the case in a sense. I read Buck's editorial and waited, along with many others perhaps, to see who would volunteer. No name appearing in the next issue of the BULLETIN, I had about decided to offer myself as a fair target when I saw Red Strauch, the '22 scribe, in Wilkes-Barre, and that clinched the matter. He seemed to be surviving under the strain so I thought I'd take a chance.

Due to the time limit for having material in for this issue being at hand at this writing, I have had no opportunity to write to anyone, so the dope appearing this month has been gathered through the usual channels, with a few additions of my own, from having run into class-mates while on the road.

Had dinner with Johnny Bertolet whose chemical nick-name is roll-cal (see Wee-Wee Ewing), and his wife a their home in Wyomissing Hills, nea Reading, and we had quite a session in the short time I could stay. He ha three fine youngsters, which, as far a I know now, constitutes the largest '2 family. (Any additional claimants fo this honor please submit data in writ ing to this address. No marriage cer tificate required.)

I attended all the bouts during th intercollegiates and saw Ray an George Childs, Mercury Locke, Harol

Heiligman, Fritz Christman and some others I can't recall now. Oh, yes, Rheiny Rheinfrank was one. Saw Sam Kaufman at the Philadelphia Club Lafayette dinner at Bookbinders last Fall, and he has his eye on an M.D. degree from Jefferson.

Both Riebe and Christman are comparatively new papas and are much wrapped up, in their families, consisting of one wife and one daughter each.

Johnny Bertolet told me he saw Ned Claxton somewhere, but neglected to say what shape he was in. Incidentally Bert is now a dispenser of black diamonds, with not much slate, assorted shapes, and is the Berks County representative for Kendall Oils. He is the largest lump of the Metropolitan Coal Co., Reading, Pa.

Norman Merkel is a partner in the drug store at 12th and Hamilton Sts., Allentown, Pa., and earnestly asks that all prescriptions be brought to him to fill. He may also fill any old bottles which you may have lying around.

Class of 1922
C. C. Strauch, Correspondent
154 E. Northampton St.,
Wilkes-Barre, Pa.

A few more fellows have come to life and exercised their right arms to the extent of giving us a little dope as to how the world is being run.

F. C. Agnew is doing sales work for the Central Rubber & Supply Co. and he is living at the Y. M. C. A., Indianapolis, Ind,

H. W. Morgan is a structural engineer with the Virginia Bridge and Iron Co. He is living at 501 Walnut Ave., S. E., Roanoke, Va.

P. O. Roberts is assistant to the manager of the advertising department of Spencer Trask & Co., at 25 Broad St., New York, N. Y., and lives at 146 N. Grove St., East Orange, N. J.

P. L. Terry now lives at 329 Park St., Hackensack, N. J.

Dutch Tavenner, who has been assistant general superintendent of Legitts Creek & Von Storch Collieries of South Pennsylvania Collieries Co., Scranton, Pa., has been transferred to the position of colliery superintendent of the Randolph Colliery, near Pottsville, Pa. He lives at the Pottsville Club and is Treasurer of the Engineers' Society of Northeastern Pennsylvania. The writer was in Pottsville a few days ago and heard that Dutch was behaving well in direct contrast to his former reputation.

Our illustrious president writes us from Pittsburgh, that he will keep us posted on any news that comes through from his end of the line. Bill started off in good shape and tells us that Bill Bowler has the Standard Oil Co. right where he wants it. Bill Little is evidently right in a nest of Lehigh men out in Pittsburgh, for he has John Hood, '21, Bill Rogers, '27, Buzz Herrington, '21, Ted Scheetz, '23, and John Marshall, '21, to check him up and keep his behavior on the right path. Bill also tells us that he has heard from some source, that Sam Shipley, '22, is working "like Hell" down in York and we are wondering how true it is.

Chubby Satterthwait has given up selling automobiles and is now taking care of the building of the big Hudson

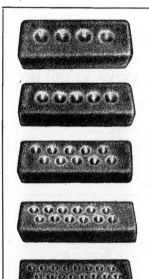
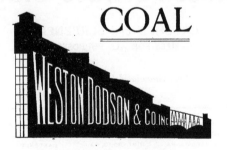

River Bridge, which is under construction at Fort Lee and Fort Washington. We don't know just how this bridge is going to make out but we can make sure that Chubby, through his connection with the McClintic-Marshall Construction Co. in Pottstown, is being checked up on most of the details in good shape. Chubby tells us he saw Ed Downing in Buffalo during the summer of 1927 but he can't tell us what has happened to Ed since then.

Class of 1923

A. C. Cusick, Correspondent
62 E. Market St., Bethlehem, Pa.

J. Brooke Buckley and his brothers have opened up a brokerage office, Philadelphia branch of Jenks-Gwynne Co., at 2031 Locust St. Baldy Stewart drove this sea-going admiral from Columbus into the field of business. Good luck, Brooke.

That sure was good news about Bloch. Keep up the good work, Elmer. I'll be looking for a job cutting your grass in a few years.

Met J. Hinkle Opdycke in Pittsburgh on Good Friday. It sure was a good Friday to see smiling Johnnie. He is with duPont Chemical Co., trying to brighten up Pittsburgh by selling the best paints ever. Can you paint a sore throat, Johnnie?

Fritz Lewis is still working for John M. Nelson, Jr., Inc., Lumber Co., of Pottsville. Still single and paying his own board and room. Get a little exercise, Fritz, and taper down a bit. Don't get too fat or you won't be able to sing at our next banquet.

Eddie Rieman is still in the engineering department of the New Jersey Zinc Co., at Palmerton, and is very happy—single.

O. F. Roller is selling lacquers, enamels, varnishes, and what have you, for Denny, Hilborn and Rosenbach, Inc., of Philadelphia. Spent Easter with Bob Platt, who, acording to Roller's report, has a very charming wife. Be careful, Bob, Roller is a shiek.

Boys, it's happened! The Psi U twins are separated. Don Quick took to himself a wife in September, 1927, and has a son, who, by the way, won't be an M.E., born March 26. Great, Don, congratulations! Let me see,—1, 2, 3,—Hell, I was always poor at math, so I can't check up on you. I'll have Eye Beam Hartung check you.

The other twin, I-Beam Hartung, is checking his drives and putts and hopes they will work out true. Don beat you to it, Phil; step on the gas and get going. Phil is test engineer at the Essex Power Station and is living at 44 Walnut St., Newark.

Jake Eckfeldt is in Santiago, Chile. Jake sailed from New York on the S. S. Santa Maria on Feb. 14 and arrived March 7. He is mining engineering salesman for the International Machinery Co., of Santiago. His address is Casilla, 107 D. In Jake's absence, his dad, Skipper, answered his card. Many thanks, Skipper.

Charlie Voss has formed a law partnership with Irving Lydecker, with offices at 76 Mamaroneck Ave., White Plains, N. Y., and 2 Rector St., New York City. Might need you soon, Charlie, with this "5 and 10" law, so get plenty of experience.

Class of 1924

5-YEAR REUNION, JUNE 8, 1929
Charles M. Alford, Correspondent
61 Glenwood Ave., East Orange, N. J.

Additional replies to about the number of a dozen have trickled in during the past month, and we gratefully acknowledge all favors. Included among those heard from is another man temporarily hiding under a basket. If the gentleman with the Irving Trust Co., 81 Fulton St., New York, will kindly forward his name, we shall be glad indeed to note his reply upon the official record.

Donald Luce is still keeping up his old comradeship with Jim Degnan. His reply did not furnish a wealth of information but in case any of you want to find him, it would be a good plan to try the Y. M. C. A. in Jersey City, N. J.

P. E. Schwartz is one of the few members of the class who has been unable to tear himself away from Bethlehem. He is living at 414 Martel St. He writes that "Figley was the only other member of the class I saw around college on February 22, when the Mid-Winter Homecoming was held."

Edwin L. Stauffer is superintendent of the gas department, South Carolina Power Co., Charleston, S. C., and living at 32 Corning St., that town. He was a little vague with information but is hoping to make the rather long trip, for him, to the reunion in June.

Frank T. Brumbaugh is living in Pittsburgh, at 120 Central Square. He is with the bureau of investigation, metallurgical department, of the Carnegie Steel Co. In his spare time he is taking graduate courses in metallurgy at Carnegie Tech.

Kenneth Donaldson thinks his chances of staying single are "excellent." Don't know why. He is in Washington, D. C., engaged in patent work, and living at 3803 Gramercy St., N. W.

W. P. Canavan, who received his Ph.D. from the University of Pennsylvania last term, had his thesis published in the April issue of the English journal *Parisitology.*

S. T. Mackenzie is living at 715 E. Wyndmoor Ave., Chestnut Hill, Philadelphia, Pa.

C. M. White is now manager of the Lehigh Telephone Co., in Bethlehem. He lives at 1719 Elm St. in this city.

E. H. Platt, whose address was lost to our records, has been located. He is with the Bureau of Investigation of the U. S. Dept. of Justice. His work consists principally of investigations of violations of the National Bank Act. He may be reached at P. O. Box 70; Wall St. Station, New York City. Since he is constantly travelling from one place to another, he has no residence address.

Ernest Baker is another member of the class religiously withstanding feminine charms. He is acting as "scoutmaster of a troop of wide awake young Indians, that is boy scouts." His address is 1520 Penn St., Harrisburg.

Class of 1925

A. L. Bayles, Correspondent
909-11 Commercial Bank Bldg.,
Charlotte, N. C.

George Paxton is assistant experimental engineer with the Pierce Arrow Motor Car Co., Buffalo, N. Y. That's a good car, too. He is now living at 780 Amherst Avenue. —

Franklin Lerch is at 45 Hitchcock Hall, University of Chicago.

H. J. Finley is clerk of the court for the City of Newark in the Newark Traffic Court. He lives at 56 Schley Street, Newark.

E. G. Ewing is with the fire engine production division of the International Motor Company, Allentown.

Max Levitz has moved to 480 Birkel Ave., Bethlehem.

This about concludes the broadcast for this period. So long until next month.

Class of 1926

As is usually the case at most functions on the campus, '26 was well represented at sub-freshman day, held on April 27. Mil. Stoffiet headed the list when he brought down a bunch of boys from Lehighton, where he is teaching in the high school.

Jimmy LeVan writes in that he is back with the Army. You probably remember how enthusiastic he was for the R. O. T. C. when in college. He is in the U. S. Engineers' Office, First District, New York City. His address is Room 702, Army Building, 39 Whitehall Street, and his job is to make studies of streams in that district for flood control. Incidentally he met a bunch of fellow civils in a "Village dive," namely: Tubs Halteman, Ken Sheppard and Lew Elliott. Jim failed to mention what kind of "streams" he was studying. His presence in a "dive" might give some indication of the kind.

Vic Schwimmer is with the bureau of private correspondence of the *Living Age*, 280 Broadway, New York. Sounds like a good job for him.

Louie Bogart is still living in Schenectady, but has deserted the G. E. Co. He is assistant auditor with the New York Power and Light Corp. at Albany.

In future years we'll be able to point to Louie Bond as one of our gang who "started at the bottom and now look at him." He claims to have started as office boy in the Christiana Machine Company and is already superintendent.

Louie has nothing on Dave Buell, who is also a "super" with the U. S. Gypsum Company in New York City.

On the other hand, Len Couch, who incidentally is on Percy Hughes' records as making one of the highest scores in the intelligence tests, has no title. He is just "with Pratt and Lambert Company" in Buffalo.

You remember Slim Griesemer started out as an austere member of the faculty at Brown but the job was too serious for jovial Slim so he returned to Allenstadt and is now an engineer in charge of proposition analysis with the Fuller Lehigh Company.

Mike Harris is another of our law students, only he has a job on the side with the Philadelphia Electric Company, in their legal department. Temple is his new Alma Mater.

Don't forget June 7 and 8. There are two more long years before our five-year reunion, so this would be a good time for an informal reunion. If you wait until 1931, you may not recognize the campus by that time.

Class of 1927

M. W. VanBilliard, Correspondent
341 W. 4th St., Bethlehem, Pa.

Dear Gang:

A large number of the fellows have dropped completely from sight and we must take means extraordinaire to discover just what has become of them. Within the next month I expect to write to each member of the class and ask a number of impertinent questions, which I hope no one will avoid. It is also time we started plans for a reunion within the next year, and took more action in regard to the Alumni Association. The records show our class to be more sluggish than the majority.

A few of the boys have written and although I have not answered each and every letter thus far, I am taking this means of expressing my thanks not only for the news items that accompanied each communication but also the "old gang" spirit that pervaded each one.

H. J. Henke, who was in the research department of the Allis Chalmers Mfg. Co., in West Allis, Wis., is now doing designing work in their Pittsburgh offices. He is living at 600 W. North Ave., Pittsburgh.

F. E. Jedlicka is an electrical engineer with the Atlas-Portland Cement Co., in Northampton, Pa. He is living at 324 N. 7th St., Allentown, Pa.

E. P. Oswald has moved to 923 Hamilton St., Allentown, Pa.

Bob Longstreet is in the district office of the N. J. Bell Tel. Co., at Asbury Park, his home town. He has already climbed to the position of district commercial sales supervisor.

E. H. Schaub is with the Barnes Mfg. Co., of Mansfield, Ohio, and is traveling as a company representative.

J. G. Ridsdale was in Bethlehem not so long ago interviewing senior chemical engineering students for the Rohm-Haas Co., of Philadelphia, for whom he is now working.

We were somewhat surprised to hear of the announcement of the engagement of Chink Roberts to Miss Madeline Rightly and must extend our congrats through these columns because of the loss of his address. How about that address so the rest of us can write before it is too late, Chink?

Toady is now in what he terms to be a "preacher factory," better known as the General Theological Seminary in New York City. He expresses himself as being greatly interested in his work and pulling down good grades—wonder of wonders. With him at G. T. S. are several other Lehigh men, among them being Gibson, '28, Jack Travis, '26, and H. W. Becker, who took a P. G. course in mining in '27. Toady is a middler and will enter the senior class next year. He extends a courteous welcome to each and every one to drop in at his abode, 175 9th Ave.

At the same time he is sending out an S.O.S. call to some of his old buddies, whom he seems to have lost track of. It is up to the following to get in touch with him: Bill and Frank Cooper, Paul Ely, and Stoddard. The only addresses that I can help you out with are these, Toady: Bill Cooper at 822 E. Dewart St.,

Shamokin, Pa.; Ely at 100 McKee Ave., Monessen, Pa., and Stoddard at 66 N. 1st St., Bangor, Pa.

An unexpected visitor to Bethlehem the other week was Johnny Knebels, who is one of the few educational students who followed his original intention of entering the teaching profession. Johnny is located in the public school system at Tenafly, N. J., and his address is 54 Magnolia Ave.

Lynch, we hear, is operating his own laundry in Pitman, N. J. Ice Schrader is a member of the Essex County engineer's staff in New Jersey. A letter will reach him if addressed to the county engineer's office in East Orange. Blaine McCarty, who weathered two seasons as the football coach of Pen Argyl high school and taught science in the interim, has given up that position to enter the business world in his home town.

Ted Rights, who is still connected with the Westinghouse people in Pittsburgh, makes frequent trips to his home in Bethlehem, the latest being during the last week in April. Paul Sinwell, since locating in Wilmington, is another familiar sight in old Bethlehem.

Bob Harrier remains wrapped up in the anthracite coal business in Pen Argyl. We should not be surprised to see Bob bringing someone with him to the next reunion, if you get what we mean.

We have heard that H. T. Martindale, Jr., is doing editorial work with the Fairchild Publications at 8 E. 13th St., New York City. H. B. Russell is assistant on the engineering corps of the P. R. R. at Wooster, Ohio, his address being 540 High St., that city. Roy F. Scholl is working at Open Hearth No. 3 of the Bethlehem Steel Co.

One of the farthest afield is G. B. Grunwell, who is employed as a field engineer with the Apure Venezuela Petroleum Corp. He can be reached at Calle del Sol 206, Valencia, Venezuela. R. Cetina will receive mail in care of the Houston Lighting and Power Co., Houston, Tex.

Chick Farrell is with the Franklin Fluorspar Co., but is now located at Rosiclare, Ill. H. P. Hebard is living at 136 Spring St., Middletown, Pa. Paul Ketterer is with the Pennsylvania Bell Telephone Co., and lives at 238 N. Negley Ave., Pittsburgh.

E. P. Kost is in the open hearth department at the Sparrows Point plant of the Bethlehem Steel Co. Forry Phillips is living at 69 W. 66th St., New York City. Rees Roderick is located with the Bethlehem Steel Co., and is living on W. Broad St., Bethlehem.

Class of 1928

1-YEAR REUNION, JUNE 8, 1929

W. B. Billmeyer, Correspondent
89-25 Parsons Blvd., Jamaica, N. Y.

Have just received a short but sweet letter from Dave Randall. As some of you know, Dave, at the beginning of the year, was attending Harvard Law School, no! he didn't bust out, only four years at Lehigh made him believe he had had enough school. Dave is now with "The Brick Row Book Shop," acting as a salesman of rare books and manuscripts. His address is 42 E. 50th St., New York City.

R. L. Mohr is now inflicting upon others what he endured for many years. He is teaching mathematics in the Paulsboro H. S., and living in Coopersburg, Pa., R. D. 1.

Ran into Ken Chickering over the week-end and he certainly does look prosperous. At present he is still working in Oil City but expects to be transferred shortly to somewhere west of the Mississippi.

Len Horton and Art Searing, two "Beau Brummels" of '28 are now working in one of the New York banks. We are led to believe that the telephone operators didn't live up to the expectations so they have forsaken the Telephone Company and are seeing what the banking game has to offer.

Leo Paley is with Holt, Rose and Troster at 74 Trinity Place, New York City. He is living at 349 Crown St., Brooklyn. Leo is assistant sales manager for his concern.

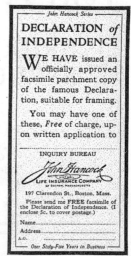

This will introduce!

INTERCOLLEGIATE ALUMNI HOTELS

Albany, N.Y., Hampton
Amherst, Mass., Lord Jeffery
Atlantic City, N.J.
    Colton Manor
Baltimore, Md., Southern
Berkeley, Cal., Claremont
Bethlehem, Pa., Bethlehem
Boothbay Harbor, Maine
    Sprucewold Lodge (summer only)
Boston, Mass., Bellevue
Chicago, Ill., Allerton House
Chicago, Ill., Blackstone
Chicago, Ill., Windermere
Cleveland, O., Allerton House
Columbus, O., Neil House
Detroit, Mich., Book-Cadillac
Elizabeth, N.J., Winfield-Scott
Fresno, Cal., Californian
Greenfield, Mass., Weldon
Jacksonville, Fla.,
    George Washington
Lexington, Ky., Phoenix
Lincoln, Neb., Lincoln
Miami, Fla., Ta-Miami

Minneapolis, Minn., Nicollet
New Brunswick, N.J.
    Woodrow Wilson
New Haven, Conn., Taft
New Orleans, La., Monteleone
New York, N.Y.,
    Fraternity Clubs Bldg.
New York, N.Y., Warwick
New York, N.Y., Westbury
Oakland, Cal., Oakland
Philadelphia, Pa.,
    Benjamin Franklin
Pittsburgh, Pa., Schenley
Providence, R.I.,
    Providence-Biltmore
Rochester, N.Y., Powers
San Francisco, Cal., Palace
Scranton, Pa., Jermyn
Spokane, Wash., Dessert
Springfield, Ill., St. Nicholas
St. Louis, Mo., New Jefferson
Syracuse, N.Y., Syracuse
Urbana, Ill., Urbana-Lincoln
Washington, D.C., Willard
Wilkes-Barre, Pa.,
    Mallow-Sterling

If you travel to any extent you should have in your possession at all times an introduction card to the managers of Intercollegiate Alumni Hotels...It is yours for the asking...It assures courteous attention to your wants and an extra bit of consideration that frequently means much.

Your alumni association is participating in the Intercollegiate Alumni Hotel Plan and has a voice in its efforts and policies. At each alumni hotel is an index of resident alumni for your convenience in looking up friends when traveling. Other desirable features are included.

If you wish an introduction card to the managers of Intercollegiate Alumni Hotels, write to your Alumni Secretary or use the coupon.

INTERCOLLEGIATE ALUMNI EXTENSION SERVICE, INC.

369 LEXINGTON AVENUE, NEW YORK, N. Y.

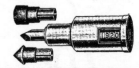